CROCKPOT RECIPES COOKBOOK

Popular, Savory and Simple Recipes to Manage Your Health

(Early Morning Recipes for the Slow Cooker)

Sandra Marden

Published by Alex Howard

© **Sandra Marden**

All Rights Reserved

Crockpot Recipes Cookbook: Popular, Savory and Simple Recipes to Manage Your Health (Early Morning Recipes for the Slow Cooker)

ISBN 978-1-990169-94-6

All rights reserved. No part of this guide may be reproduced in any form without permission in writing from the publisher except in the case of brief quotations embodied in critical articles or reviews.

Legal & Disclaimer

The information contained in this book is not designed to replace or take the place of any form of medicine or professional medical advice. The information in this book has been provided for educational and entertainment purposes only.

The information contained in this book has been compiled from sources deemed reliable, and it is accurate to the best of the Author's knowledge; however, the Author cannot guarantee its accuracy and validity and cannot be held liable for any errors or omissions. Changes are periodically made to this book. You must consult your doctor or get professional medical advice before using any of the suggested remedies, techniques, or information in this book.

Table of contents

Part 1 1

Introduction 2

SLOW COOKER SOUPS AND STEWS 3

Sausage barley soup 3

Spicy beef curry stew 4

Spicy slow cooker black bean soup 6

Chicken pot pie stew 7

Beef vegetable soup 8

Grandma B's bean soup 10

Winter lentil vegetable soup 11

SLOW COOKER SIDE DISHES 13

Garlic mashed potatoes 13

Sweet potato casserole 14

Creamed spinach 15

Risotto 16

Risi bisi 17

Cheesy potatoes 18

Wild rice casserole 19

The best slow cooker cream corn 20

Creamed corn 21

Stuffing for slow cooker 21

SLOW COOKER SAUCES 23

All night apple butter 23

Stephanie's freezer spaghetti sauce 24

Apple peach sauce 25

Tangy horseradish tomato sauce for meatballs 25

Reduced sugar spiced apple butter 26

SLOW COOKER MAIN DISHES 27

Macaroni and cheese 27

Fruit, nuts and spice oatmeal 28

Pot roast dips 29

Lime chicken with rice 30

Buffalo chicken sandwiches 31

Marie's easy slow cooker pot roast 31

Beef stroganoff 32

London broil 33

Daria's slow cooker beef stroganoff 34

SLOW COOKER DESSERTS 35

Bread pudding 35

Unbelievably easy slow cooker black forest cake 36

Tapioca pudding 37

Apple tapioca pudding 37

Cherry cobbler 38

Apple brown betty 39

Apples with cinnamon and brown sugar 40

Peach cobbler 41

Tapioca pudding 42

Strawberry slow cooker scoop cake 42

Apple cinnamon bread pudding 43

SLOW COOKER APPETIZERS 44

Hot roasted red pepper and artichoke dip 44

Spicy hot chicken legs 45

Vegetarian buffalo chicken dip 46

Marinated mushrooms 46

Healthier buffalo chicken dip 47

Easy marinated mushrooms 48

Cheese dip 49

Famous meatballs 50

Slow-Cooker Easy Chicken Alfredo 52

Slow Cooker Spaghetti and Meatballs 54

Slow Cooker Pot Roast 56

Slow Cooker Chicken Taco Soup 57

Slow Cooker Chicken and Dumplings 59

Slow Cooker Italian Beef for Sandwiches 61

Slow Cooker Mexican Style Meat 63

Slow Cooker Chicken Barbecue 65

Slow Cooker Ribs 66

Slow Cooker Rabbit Stew 68

Slow Cooker Beef Shank 70

Slow Cooker Chicken Tortilla Soup 72

Slow Cooker Salisbury Steak 74

Slow-Cooker Chicken Burrito Bowls 76

Slow-Cooker Enchilada Meatballs 78

Conclusion 80

Part 2 81

Introduction 82

Paleo Egg and Nut Bread 83

Honey Glazed Shrimp 84

Squash Bake 86

Almond Honey Chicken Dippers 88

Paleo Pineapple & Walnut Applesauce 90

Cinnamon Pumpkin Soup 91

Paleo Sweet & Sour Cabbage 92

Immune Boosting Chicken Soup 93

Paleo Brownies 95

Squash, Broccoli, and Cauliflower Bake 96

Spicy Sausage, Basil and Eggs 98

Spiced Chicken Kabobs on a Bed of Cabbage 99

Fiery Beef, Asparagus, and Brussel Sprouts 101

Squash and Sausage in Mushroom Gravy 103

Paleo Jambalaya 104

Paleo Spinach and Kale 106

Pearl Onions and Spinach 107

Paleo Crockpot Sweet Onions 109

Paleo Bacon Bake 110

Eggplant & Ham Ragu 112

Chicken & Ginger Casserole 114

Apple & Cinnamon Stuffed Peppers 115

Cauliflower Stuffed Peppers 117

Zucchini Lasagna 119

Veggie Ragu 121

Squash Chili 122

Zesty Turkey Chili 124

Curried Collards 126

Noodles Soup 127

Squash Casserole 128

Okra Soup 129

Spicy Cabbage and Onions 130

Caramelized Onions 131

Fall Spice Applesauce 132

Grilled Salmon and Pomegranate Mint Applesauce 133

Cauliflower Rice & Chicken Casserole 135

Zucchini Noodle Slow Cooker Mac and Cheese 136

Slow Cooker Paleo Enchiladas 138

Paleo Seafood Delight 139

Spicy Autumn Stew 141

Paleo Cucumber Pasta and Strawberries 142

Pumpkin Soup 144

Paleo Crockpot Chicken Casserole	145
5-Step Paleo Chicken Nugget's	146
Tangy Mango Sauce	147
Paleo Tacos	149
Salmon Salsa	151
Spinach and Mushroom in Squash Bowls	153
Paleo Asparagus Ragu	154
Paleo Chicken Kabobs and Kiwi Salad	155
Salsa Verde Chicken	157
Balsamic Beef & Carrots	159
Shrimp & Noodles	161
Chicken Teriyaki	163
Crockpot Curried Chicken	165
Spring Thyme Chicken Stew	167
Chicken Santa Fe	169
Jackfruit Stew	171
This vegetarian stew is rich, and delicious.	171
Coconut Chicken Soup	173
Vietnamese Beef Curry Stew	175
Basil Tofu	177

Pork Stew 179

Almond Spiced Beef 181

Turkey Meatballs 183

Spicy Chicken Stew 185

Crockpot Ribs 186

Part 1

Introduction

Often after a hard day of work, you come home only to discover that you still have to cook food. Preparing several ingredients, and then cooking can be complicated, time-consuming and you may decide to skip dinner altogether. If you are you are looking for an easy solution, short on time but crave for healthy, home-cooked meals then this cookbook on fast slow cooker recipes is for you. No matter if it's a hectic weeknight or a rushed morning, slow cooker guarantees delicious meals all the time, every night.

With these slow cooker recipes, you can eat healthy food every night of the week. A slow cooker can save you time, energy and money. All you have to do is prepare your meals and freeze it in a bag, and preparation of 15 meals will take only 1 hour of your time, and provide you and your family with a 2-week priory prepared dinner or lunch. Whenever you have to eat, just take out the bag of food from a freezer and put everything in it to cook in a slow cooker. No prepping, no mess, no time wasting. This cookbook on slow cooker revolution: easy freeze-ahead will make your life enjoyable and hassle free. The recipes in this book will make it possible for you to spend more time with your family and less time in the kitchen. Take back your time and discover how this slow cooker cookbook will make your life easier for you. This cookbook is a must have for health-conscious families and busy professionals.

SLOW COOKER SOUPS AND STEWS

Sausage barley soup

Ingredients
- Beef sausage (1 pound)
- Chicken broth (1 can or 48 fluid ounce)
- Diced onion (½ cup)
- 1 large carrot, sliced
- Minced garlic (1 tbsp)
- Frozen chopped spinach (1 package or 10 ounces)

- Italian seasoning (½ tsp)

- **Uncooked pearl barley (¼ cup)**

Directions

Place skillet on the stove and cook garlic, onion and sausage over medium heat until sausage brown. Flavor it with Italian seasoning.

Take away from the stove and drain.

Mix barley, spinach, carrot, chicken broth and sausage mixture together in a slow cooker.

Cover and cook on high for about 4 hours.

Spicy beef curry stew

Ingredients
- Olive oil (1 tbsp)
- 1 fresh jalapeno peppers, diced

- Beef stew meat (1 pound)
- Curry powder (1 tbsp)
- Pepper and salt to taste
- Diced tomatoes with juice (1 can or 14.5 ounce)
- 2 cloves garlic, minced
- 1 onion, sliced and quartered
- Chopped fresh ginger (1 tsp)

- **Beef broth (1 cup)**

Directions
Place skillet on the stove and heat olive oil in it.
Fry beef until brown and flavor it with pepper and salt.
Cook jalapeno, ginger and garlic for about 2 minutes with constant stirring until tender and flavor it with curry powder. Mix in juice and diced tomatoes.
Take slow cooker, put in onion along with brown beef.
Add beef broth and skillet mixture.
Cover and cook on low for about 6-8 hours.

Spicy slow cooker black bean soup

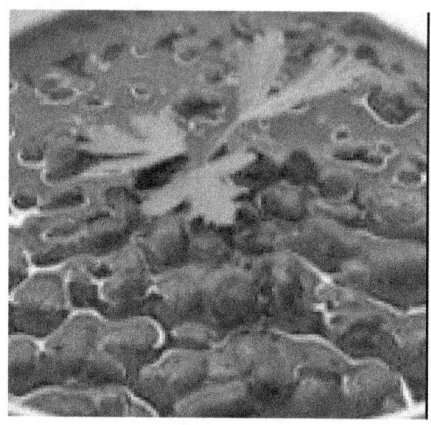

Ingredients
- Dry black beans (1 pound), soaked overnight
- Ground cumin (1 tsp)
- Diced jalapeno peppers (4 tsp)
- Cayenne pepper (1 tsp)
- Chicken broth (6 cups)
- Ground black pepper (¾ tsp)
- Garlic powder (½ tsp)
- Hot pepper sauce (½ tsp)

- **Chili powder (1 tbsp)**

Directions
Drain black beans and wash.

Take slow cooker; combine chicken broth, jalapenos and beans together.

Flavor it with hot pepper sauce, pepper, cayenne, cumin, chili powder and garlic powder.

Cook for about 4 hours on high. Minimize the heat and cook for about 2 hours on low until ready.

Chicken pot pie stew

Ingredients
- 4 large skinless, boneless chicken breast halves, cut into cubes
- Chicken bouillon (6 cubes)
- 10 medium red potatoes, quartered
- Garlic salt (2 tsp)

- Celery salt (1 tsp)
- Ground black pepper (1 tbsp)
- Baby carrots (1 package or 8 ounce)
- Chopped celery (1 cup)
- Frozen mixed vegetables (1 bag or 16 ounce)

- **Condensed cream of chicken soup (2 cans or 26 ounces)**

Directions

Take slow cooker and combine celery salt, garlic salt, black pepper, chicken bouillon, chicken soup, celery, carrots, potatoes and chicken together and cook for about 5 hours on high.

Put frozen mixed vegetable and cook further for an hour.

Beef vegetable soup

Ingredients
- Cubed beef stew meat (1 pound)
- Sliced potatoes with juice (1 can or 15 ounce)
- Whole kernel corn (1 can or 15.25 ounce), undrained
- Crushed tomatoes (1 can or 28 ounce)
- Green beans (1 can or 15 ounce)
- Beef with onion soup mix (1 package or 1.25 ounce)
- Carrots with juice (1 can or 15 ounce)

- **Pepper and salt to taste**

Directions
Combine soup mix, tomatoes, potatoes, carrots, green beans, corn and meat together in a slow cooker and flavor it with pepper and salt.
Cook for about 6 hours on low and then serve.

Grandma B's bean soup

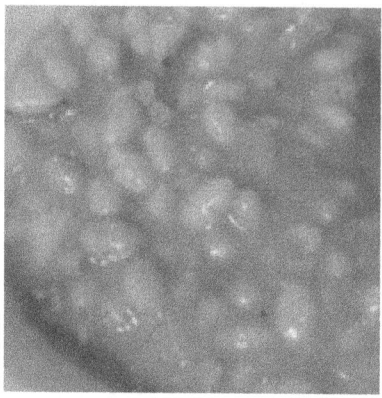

Ingredients
- Dry navy beans (1 pound)
- 3 stalks celery, sliced
- 3 carrots, peeled and shredded
- 1 medium onion, diced
- 2 medium potatoes, peeled and diced

- **Beef stew meat (1 pound)**

Directions
Put beans along with water in a slow cooker and soak overnight.
Drain beans and put it back along with water. Mix in beef, onion, celery, potatoes and carrots.
Cover and cook for about 3 hours on high.
Then reduce to low and cook for about 6 hours.

Serve!

Winter lentil vegetable soup

Ingredients
- Green lentil (½ cup)
- 1 clove garlic, crushed
- Chopped onion (1 cup)
- Salt (1 tsp)
- 1 stalk celery, chopped
- Ground black pepper (½ tsp)
- Shredded cabbage (2 cups)
- White sugar (¼ tsp)
- Whole peeled tomatoes (1 can or 28 ounce), chopped
- Dried basil (½ tsp)
- Chicken broth (2 cups)
- Dried thyme (½ tsp)

- 3 carrots, chopped

- **Curry powder (¼ tsp)**

Directions
Dip lentils in water in a stockpot and boil.
Minimize the heat and cook for about 15 minutes.
Take out, wash and put it back to the pot.
Put in garlic, carrots, chicken broth, tomatoes, cabbage, celery and onions.
Flavor with curry, thyme, basil, sugar, pepper and salt and cook for about 2 hours until tender.
Serve!

SLOW COOKER SIDE DISHES

Garlic mashed potatoes

Ingredients
- Red potatoes (2 pounds), diced with peel
- Garlic powder (½ tsp)
- Water (¼ cup)
- Ground black pepper (¼ tsp)
- Butter (¼ cup)
- Milk (½ cup)

- **Salt (1 ¼ tsp)**

Directions

Take slow cooker put butter, water and potatoes in it and flavor with pepper, salt and garlic powder. Cover and cook for about 4 hours on high.

Grind potatoes, add milk and achieve desired consistency.

Heat on low and then serve.

Sweet potato casserole

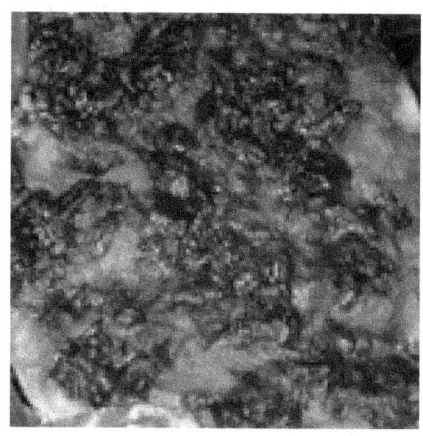

Ingredients
- Sweet potatoes (2 cans or 29 ounces), drained and grinded
- Milk (½ cup)
- Butter (1/3 cup), melted
- Chopped pecans (1/3 cup)

- White sugar (2 tbsp)
- Brown sugar (1/3 cup)
- Brown sugar (2 tbsp)
- Whole flour (2 tbsp)
- Orange juice (1 tbsp)
- Butter (2 tsp), melted

- **2 eggs, beaten**

Directions
Take slow cooker and lightly grease it.
Blend brown sugar (2 tbsp), white sugar, butter (1/3 cup) and sweet potatoes in a large bowl. Beat in milk, eggs and orange juice and shift to the casserole dish.
Combine butter (2 tsp), flour and the remaining 1/3 cup of brown sugar in a small bowl.
Add this mixture to casserole dish, cover and cook for about 3-4 hours on high and then serve.

Creamed spinach

Ingredients
- Frozen chopped spinach (2 packages or 10 ounces), thawed, drained and squeezed dry

- Cubed process cheese (1 ½ cups)
- Cheddar cheese (2 cups)
- Whole flour (¼ cup)
- Butter (½ cup), cubed
- Salt (1 tsp)

- **3 eggs, beaten**

Directions
Mix flour, salt, eggs, cheese, butter, cheddar cheese and spinach together in a bowl until distributed uniformly.
Grease the slow cooker and transfer the mixture to it.
Cook for about an hour on high and then minimize heat and cook for about 4-5 on low.
Serve!

Risotto

Ingredients
- Chicken broth (3 ¾ cups)
- Dried onion flakes (1 tsp)
- Arborio rice (1 ¼ cups)
- Salt (1 tsp)

- Olive oil (¼ cup)
- Ground black pepper (¼ tsp)
- White vinegar (¼ cup)
- Shredded cheddar cheese (2/3 cup)

- **4 cloves garlic, minced**

Directions

Take slow cooker and mix black pepper, salt, onion flakes, garlic, vinegar, olive oil, rice and chicken broth together and cook for about 2 hours on high.

Put in cheddar cheese and cook uncovered for about 15 minutes until the cheese has melted.

Risi bisi

Ingredients
- Converted long-grain white rice (1 ½ cups)
- Italian seasoning (¾ tsp)
- Chopped onion (1/3 cup)
- Dried basil (½ tsp)
- 2 cloves garlic, chopped
- Frozen green peas (½ cup), thawed
- Chicken broth (2 cans or 14 ounce)

- Cheddar cheese (¼ cup)
- Water (1/3 cup)

- **Pine nuts (¼ cup), toasted**

Directions
Take slow cooker and combine garlic, onion and rice in it.
Boil water and chicken broth in a skillet over high heat.
Stir basil, Italian seasoning and boiling liquid into rice mixture and cook for about 2-3 hours on low.
Put in peas, cover and cook further for about 1 hour.
Add cheese, transfer to serving dish and splash with pine nuts.

Cheesy potatoes

Ingredients
- Frozen southern-style hash brown potatoes (1 package or 32 ounce)
- Evaporated milk (1 can or 12 fluid ounce)
- **French fried onions (1 can or 2.8 ounce)**

Directions

Grease slow cooker with cooking spray.

Stir evaporated milk, half of fried onions and hash browns together in a large bowl and transfer it to slow cooker.

Cover and cook for about 4 hours on high and then splash with the reserved onions.

Serve!

Wild rice casserole

Ingredients
- 2 onions, finely chopped
- Condensed cream of mushroom soup (1 can or 10.75 ounce)
- 3 celery, thinly sliced
- Butter (½ cup)
- Dry instant long grain and wild rice mix (2 packages or 6 ounces)
- Processed cheese (½ pound)
- Water (2 ½ cups)
- **Sliced fresh mushrooms (½ cup)**

Directions
Put mushrooms, cheese, butter, mushroom soup, water, rice mix, celery and onions together in a slow cooker. Cover and cook for about 2-4 hours on high.

The best slow cooker cream corn

Ingredients
- White sugar (½ cup)
- Frozen corn kernels (4 package or 16 ounces)
- Cream cheese (3 packages or 8 ounces), cubed
- Cheese (6 slices)
- Butter (1 cup), cut into pieces
- **Whole milk (½ cup)**

Directions
Combine milk, cheese, sugar, butter, cream cheese and corn together in a slow cooker.
Cover and cook on low for about 3 hours and stir after every 30 minutes.

Creamed corn

Ingredients
- Milk (½ cup)
- Frozen corn kernels (1 ¼ package or 16 ounces)
- White sugar (1 tbsp)
- Cream cheese (1 package or 8 ounce)
- Pepper and salt to taste

- **Butter (½ cup)**

Directions
Combine sugar, milk, butter, cream cheese and corn together in a slow cooker and flavor it with pepper and salt.
Cook for 2-4 hours on high and then serve.

Stuffing for slow cooker

Ingredients
- Butter (1 cup)
- Dried thyme (1 tsp)

- Chopped celery (2 cups)
- Sage (1 ½ tsp)
- Chopped onion (2 cups)
- Ground black pepper (½ tsp)
- Chopped parsley (¼ cup)
- Salt (1 ½ tsp)
- Mushrooms (2 cans or 8 ounce), drained
- Dried marjoram (½ tsp) [optional]
- White bread (12 cups), cut into cubes
- 2 eggs, beaten
- Poultry seasoning (1 tsp)
- **Chicken broth (4 cups)**

Directions

Melt butter in a saucepan over medium heat and fry mushrooms, parsley, celery and onion until the onions are tender.

Combine vegetables and bread cubes in a large bowl. Put in marjoram, salt, pepper, sage, thyme and poultry seasoning and toss well.

Put eggs and moisten with broth.

Transfer the mixture to slow cooker and cook for about 45 minutes on high.

Minimize the heat and cook further for 4-6 hours.

SLOW COOKER SAUCES

All night apple butter

Ingredients
- Apples (8 pounds), peeled, cored and sliced
- Ground cloves (½ tsp)
- White sugar (1 cup)
- Salt (¼ tsp)
- Brown sugar (1 cup)
- Water (2 tsp)
- Ground cinnamon (1 tbsp)
- **Ground nutmeg (½ tsp)**

Directions
Take slow cooker and put apples in it.
Take bowl and stir together salt, cloves, nutmeg, cinnamon, brown sugar and white sugar.
Shift this mixture to slow cooker and sprinkle with enough water.
Cook for about 10 hours on low. Serve and enjoy.

Stephanie's freezer spaghetti sauce

Ingredients
- 4 onions, chopped
- Dried basil (2 tbsp)
- 4 cloves garlic, minced
- Chopped parsley (¼ cup)
- 1 green bell pepper, chopped
- White sugar (¼ cup)
- Vegetable oil (½ cup)
- Salt (2 tbsp)
- Chopped tomatoes (16 cups)
- Ground black pepper (¾ tsp)
- Dried oregano (2 tbsp)

- **Tomato paste (1 can or 6 ounce)**

Directions
Saute vegetable oil, green pepper, garlic and onion together in a slow cooker and cook until onions are tender.
Add ground black pepper, salt, sugar, parsley, basil, oregano and chopped tomatoes and cook on low for 2-3 hours, stirring often.
Let it stand for some time to cool. After cooling transfer it to the container and store in freezer.
Add tomato paste before using.

Apple peach sauce

Ingredients
- Ground cinnamon (1 tbsp)
- 4 fresh peaches, pitted and chopped
- **10 Macintosh apples, cored and chopped**

Directions
Take slow cooker and put fruit in it.
Splash with cinnamon, cover and cook on high for about 3 hours.
Then turn to low and further cook for about 2 hours.
Stir and then serve.

Tangy horseradish tomato sauce for meatballs

Ingredients
- Condensed tomato soup (1 can or 10.75 ounce)
- Mustard (1 tbsp)
- Garlic powder (2 tsp)
- Tomato-vegetable juice cocktail (1 can or 46 ounce)

- Steak sauce (3 tbsp)
- Black pepper (¼ tsp)
- Dried onion flakes (¼ cup)
- Instant tapioca (3 tbsp)
- Dried parsley (2 tbsp)
- Water (2 cups)

- **Horseradish prepared in white vinegar (2 tbsp)**

Directions

Take slow cooker and mix tapioca, water, black pepper, garlic powder, mustard, horseradish, dried parsley, onion flakes, Steak sauce, vegetable juice cocktail and tomato soup together.

Cook for about 3-4 hours on low until thickened.

Reduced sugar spiced apple butter

Ingredients
- Apples (4 pounds), coarsely chopped
- Ground cinnamon (4 tsp)
- Brown sugar (½ cup)
- Ground cloves (½ tsp)
- Vinegar (¼ cup)

- **Salt (½ tsp)**

Directions

Take slow cooker and stir cloves, salt, cinnamon, vinegar, brown sugar and chopped apples together. Cook on low for about 8 hours until apples are tender. Blend apple mixture and cook uncovered for about 1 hour until the color turns brown and liquid reduces.

SLOW COOKER MAIN DISHES

Macaroni and cheese

Ingredients
- Butter (2 tbsp)
- Evaporated milk (2 cups)
- Paprika (½ tsp)
- Cubed cheddar cheese (3 ½ cups)
- Salt (1 tsp)
- Macaroni (1 package or 8 ounce)

- **1 egg, beaten**

Directions

Combine cheese, butter, egg, salt, paprika and evaporated milk together in a slow cooker.

Boil slightly salted water in a large pot and cook macaroni in it for about 8 minutes until tender.

Stir macaroni to slow cooker, minimize the heat and cook for about 3-5 hours on low.

Fruit, nuts and spice oatmeal

Ingredients
- Steel cut oats (2 cups)
- Water (3 cups)
- Diced apple (2 cups)
- Milk (1 cup)
- Dried cranberries (1 cup)
- Ground cinnamon (1 tbsp)
- Slivered almonds (½ cup)
- Pumpkin pie spice (1 tsp)
- Chopped pecans (½ cup)

- **Butter (2 tsp)**

Directions

Combine butter, pumpkin pie spice, cinnamon, milk, water, pecans, almonds, cranberries, apple and oats together in a slow cooker and cook for about 8 hours on low.

Pot roast dips

Ingredients
- Water (1 cup)
- Beef chuck roast (2 pounds)
- Dry onion soup mix (1 package or 0.9 ounce)
- 12 hoagie rolls, split lengthwise
- Dry au jus mix (1 packet or 1 ounce)
- **Shredded mozzarella cheese (1 package or 8 ounce)**

Directions
Take slow cooker and stir onion soup, au jus and water together.
Put in beef, cover and cook for about 5 hours on high until tender.
Shred the beef and cook further for about 1-2 hours on low.
Open the split buns, add meat and splash with mozzarella cheese before serving.

Lime chicken with rice

Ingredients
- Chicken breast halves (1 ¼ pounds), skinless and boneless
- Dried thyme leaves (½ tsp)
- Lime juice (1/3 cup)
- Ground black pepper (¼ tsp)
- Chicken broth (2 cups)
- Butter (2 tbsp)
- 1 clove garlic, minced

- **Uncooked instant rice (2 cups)**

Directions
Combine chicken breast, chicken stock, lime juice, butter, pepper, thyme and garlic together in a slow cooker.
Cover and cook for about 8-10 until the chicken is tender.
Add rice and cook further for about 15 minutes.

Buffalo chicken sandwiches

Ingredients
- 4 skinless, boneless chicken breast halves
- Butter (2 tbsp)
- Hot sauce (1 bottle or 17.5 ounce)
- 6 hoagie rolls, split lengthwise

- **Italian salad dressing (½ package or 1 ounce)**

Directions
Take slow cooker and put chicken breast in it.
Add dressing mix and ¾ of the sauce and cover.
Cook for about 6 hours on low until cooked.
Put in butter and cut the meat by using fork.
Scatter meat on the hoagie and sprinkle with the reserved sauce before serving.

Marie's easy slow cooker pot roast

Ingredients
- Chuck roast (4 pounds)
- 3 carrots, chopped

- Pepper and salt to taste
- 1 onion, chopped
- Dry onion soup mix (1 packet)
- 3 potatoes, peeled and cubed
- Water (1 cup)

- **1 stalk celery, chopped**

Directions
Take skillet and heat chuck roast for about 4 minutes in it until brown.
Flavor it with pepper and salt.
Shift the roast to slow cooker and add celery, potatoes, carrots, water, soup mix and onion.
Cover and cook for about 8 hours on low heat.

Beef stroganoff

Ingredients
- Cubed beef stew meat (1 pound)
- Steak sauce (1 tbsp)
- Condensed golden mushroom soup (1 can or 10.75 ounce)
- Water (¼ cup)
- Chopped onion (½ cup)

- **Cream cheese (4 ounces)**

Directions
Combine Steak sauce, water, onion soup and meat together in a slow cooker and cook for about 5 hours on high.
Put in cream cheese and serve.

London broil

Ingredients
- Flank steak (2 pounds)
- Condensed tomato soup (1 can or 10.75 ounce)
- Condensed cream of mushroom soup (1 can or 10.75 ounce)
- **Dry onion soup mix (1 package or 1 ounce)**

Directions
Take cooker and put in meat.
Mix soup, tomato and mushroom together in a medium bowl and transfer it to the slow cooker.
Splash dry onion soup over it and cook for about 8 hours on low.

Daria's slow cooker beef stroganoff

Ingredients
- Top round steak (1 ½ pounds), cut into strips
- 1 clove garlic, minced
- Pepper and salt to taste
- Steak sauce (1 tsp)
- ½ onion, chopped
- 1 cube beef bouillon
- Condensed cream of mushroom soup (1 can or 10.75 ounce)
- White vinegar (¼ cup)
- Whole purpose flour (1 tbsp)
- Canned mushrooms (1 can or 8 ounce)
- Sour cream (1 container or 16 ounce)
- Water (¼ cup)
- Chopped fresh parsley (½ cup)

- **Dried chives (1 tbsp)**

Directions
Take slow cooker, put in beef and flavor it with pepper and salt.

Put onions on the top and then stir water, mushroom soup and mushroom and flavor with bouillon, Steak sauce, garlic and chives.

Mix vinegar with flour together in a bowl, pour it over beef and cook for about 6 hours.

Add parsley and sour cream and cook further for 1 hour.

SLOW COOKER DESSERTS

Bread pudding

Ingredients
- Cubed bread (8 cups)
- Butter (¼ cup), melted
- Raisins (1 cup) [optional]
- White sugar (¼ cup)
- Milk (2 cups)
- 4 eggs
- **Ground nutmeg (¼ tsp)**

Directions
Take slow cooker and put raisins and bread in it.

Take bowl and whisk nutmeg, sugar, butter, eggs and milk together and toss until coat uniformly.
Cook for about 3 hours on low and then serve.

Unbelievably easy slow cooker black forest cake

Ingredients

- Butter (½ cup)
- Cheery pie filling (1 can or 21 ounce)
- Crushed pineapple (1 can or 8 ounce), drained and juiced reserved
- **Chocolate cake mix (1 package or 18.25 ounce)**

Directions
Take skillet and melt butter in it. Mix in pineapple juice and then reserve.
Scatter crushed pineapple in slow cooker in the form of layers.
Stir cherry pie filling on each layer and then add chocolate cake mix.

Mix pineapple juice and butter and transfer it to the slow cooker.

Cook for about 3 hours on low and let it stand for some time to cool before serving.

Tapioca pudding

Ingredients
- Whole milk (½ gallon)
- 4 eggs, beaten
- White sugar (1 1/3 cups)
- **Small pearl tapioca (1 cup)**

Directions
Take slow cooker and stir eggs, tapioca, sugar and milk together in it.
Cook for about 6 hours and stir after every 60 minutes.

Apple tapioca pudding

Ingredients

- Apples (4 cups), peeled, cored and sliced
- Small pearl tapioca (2 tbsp)
- Brown sugar (½ cup)
- 1 lemon, juiced
- Ground cinnamon (¾ tsp)
- Boiling water (1 cup)
- Salt (½ tsp)

- **Raisins (½ cup) [optional]**

Directions

Take bowl and put tapioca, salt, cinnamon, brown sugar and apples in it.

Toss until apple slices are coat.

Transfer the above mixture to slow cooker. Add boiling water and lemon juice and cook for about 3 hours on high until apples are tender.

Add raisins and serve hot.

Cherry cobbler

Ingredients
- Salt (¼ tsp)
- Cherry pie filling (1 can or 21 ounce)
- Butter (¼ cup), melted
- Whole flour (1 cup)
- Milk (½ cup)

- White sugar (¼ cup)
- **Baking powder (1 ½ tsp)**

Directions

Grease the cooker with cooking spray and add cherry pie filling.

Stir salt, baking powder, sugar and flour together in a bowl, make well in it. Add milk and melted butter.

Mix well, pour it over cherry pie filling and cook for about one and a half hour.

Apple brown betty

Ingredients
- Salt (1/8 tsp)
- Apples (3 cups), peeled, cored and diced
- Brown sugar (¾ cup)
- 10 slices bread, cubed
- Butter (½ cup), melted
- Ground cinnamon (½ tsp)
- **Ground nutmeg (¼ tsp)**

Directions
Take slow cooker and add apples.
Toss brown sugar, salt, nutmeg, cinnamon and bread cubes together in a bowl.
Scatter the above mixture over apple and moisten with melted butter.
Cover and cook until apples are tender.

Apples with cinnamon and brown sugar

Ingredients
- Butter (1 tbsp), chopped
- 4 medium tart baking apples, cored
- Ground cinnamon (½ tsp)
- Regular rolled oats (¼ cup)
- Raisins (¼ cup)
- Apple juice (2/3 cup)

- **Packed brown sugar (2 tbsp)**

Directions
Take slow cooker and add apples to it.
Combine cinnamon, butter, brown sugar, raisins and oats together in a small bowl. Add on the top center of

the apple patting with spatula and pour the juice around it.
Cook until the apples are tender, for 3 hours and moisten with cooking liquid.

Peach cobbler

Ingredients
- Old-fashioned oats (¾ cup)
- All-purpose baking mix (½ cup)
- White sugar (¾ cup)
- Ground cinnamon (¾ tsp)
- Brown sugar (2/3 cup)

- **5 fresh peaches – peeled, pitted and sliced**

Directions
Grease the slow cooker.
Take bowl and mix cinnamon, baking mix, brown sugar, white sugar and oats together.
Add peaches, transfer the mixture to the slow cooker and cook for about 4 hours on low.

Tapioca pudding

Ingredients
- Milk (4 cups)
- Small pearl tapioca (½ cup)
- White sugar (2/3 cup)

- **2 eggs, lightly beaten**

Directions
Take slow cooker, stir eggs, tapioca, sugar and milk together and cover.
Cook and stir for about 3 hours on medium and serve hot.

Strawberry slow cooker scoop cake

Ingredients
- Strawberry pie filling (1 can or 21 ounce)
- Melted butter (½ cup)
- Strawberry cake mix (1 package or 18.25 ounce)

- **White chocolate baking pieces (½ cup)**

Directions

Take slow cooker and put strawberry pie filling in it.
Combine butter and dry cake mix and splash pie filling over it.
Cover, cook for about 2 hours and splash with chocolate pieces.
Decorate with whipped cream and serve.

Apple cinnamon bread pudding

Ingredients
- Packed brown sugar (¾ cup)
- 4 granny smith apples – peeled, cored and chopped
- Ground cinnamon (2 tsp)
- 1 inch bread cubes (3 cups)
- Nutmeg (1 tsp)
- 4 large eggs

- **Evaporated skim milk (2 cans or 12 fluid ounces)**

Directions
Take slow cooker and combine bread and apples in it.

Take bowl, beat eggs together in it and add cinnamon, brown sugar and milk.

Pour the above mixture over bread and apples and cook for about 3 hours until custard forms.

SLOW COOKER APPETIZERS

Hot roasted red pepper and artichoke dip

Ingredients
- Cream cheese (2 package or 8 ounce), softened
- Roasted red pepper in oil with garlic (1 jar or 12 ounce), drained and chopped
- Sour cream (1 ½ cups)
- Artichoke hearts (1 jar or 6 ounce), drained and chopped
- Mayonnaise (½ cup)
- 1 loaf Italian bread, sliced
- **Mozzarella cheese (2 cups), divided**

Directions
Take large bowl and mix mayonnaise, sour cream and cream cheese together by using electric mixer until smooth.

Put in artichoke hearts, half of the mozzarella cheese and red peppers and shift to a slow cooker.

Splash reserved mozzarella on it and cook on low for about 2-3 hours until the dip is bubbly and the cheese has melted.

Serve along with bread slices.

Spicy hot chicken legs

Ingredients
- 12 Chicken drumsticks
- Onion powder (½ tsp)
- Hot red pepper sauce (1 bottle or 5 ounce)
- Pepper and salt to taste
- Butter (¼ cup), cubed

- **Italian salad dressing (1 ½ cups)**

Directions

Take slow cooker, put drumstick and splash with butter uniformly.

Add hot sauce and flavor with pepper, salt, onion powder and garlic powder.

Cover and cook for about 3 hours on high.

Serve with dressing.

Vegetarian buffalo chicken dip

Ingredients
- Seasoned chicken-style vegetarian strips (1 package or 8 ounce)
- Hot sauce (1 bottle or 12 fluid ounce)
- Reduced fat cream cheese (2 package or 8 ounce), softened
- Mozzarella-cheddar cheese blend (1 cup)
- **Italian salad dressing (1 bottle or 16 ounce)**

Directions
Put sauce, dressing, cream cheese and diced vegetarian chicken strips in slow cooker and cook for about an hour or 2 until the cheese has melted.
Put in shredded cheese before serving.

Marinated mushrooms

Ingredients
- Chicken bouillon (4 cubes)
- Steak sauce (1 tsp)
- Beef bouillon (4 cubes)
- Garlic powder (1 tsp)
- Boiling water (2 cups)
- Fresh mushrooms (4 pounds)
- Red vinegar (1 cup)
- Butter (½ cup)

- **Dill weed (1 tsp)**

Directions
Take boiling water in a pot and dissolve beef bouillon cubes and chicken in it.
Put garlic powder, Steak sauce, red vinegar and dill and stir.
Put mushrooms in slow cooker and pour the above dressing over it.
Splash with butter and cook for about 12 hours on low.

Healthier buffalo chicken dip

Ingredients

- Italian style salad dressing (1 cup)
- Multi-grain crackers (8 ounces)
- Cheese (2 packages or 8 ounces)
- 1 bunch celery, cut into pieces
- Hot pepper sauce (¾ cup)
- Shredded reduced-fat cheddar cheese (1 cup), divided
- **Natural chunk chicken (2 can or 10 ounces), drained**

Directions
Take saucepan and heat hot pepper sauce and chicken for about 5 minutes in it.
Put in dressing and cheese and cook further for 5 minutes with constant stirring until blended.
Combine half cup of cheddar cheese and shift along with the mixture to slow cooker.
Splash over cheddar cheese and cook for about half hour until bubbly and hot.
Serve with crackers and celery sticks.

Easy marinated mushrooms

Ingredients

- White sugar (2 cups)
- Soy sauce (2 cups)
- Water (2 cups)
- Fresh mushrooms (4 packages or 8 ounces), remove stems

- **Butter (1 cup)**

Directions
Place the skillet on the stove and mix butter, water and soy sauce in it.
Melt the butter by heating and then slowly add sugar until dissolved.
Take slow cooker, put mushrooms and pour the above mixture over it.
Cook for about 8 hours, stirring occasionally and refrigerate before serving.

Cheese dip

Ingredients
- Processed cheese (1 loaf or 2 pound), cubed
- Taco seasoning (1 package or 1.25 ounce)
- Ground beef (1 ½ pounds)
- Hot sauce (1 jar or 16 ounce)

- **Water (2/3 cup)**

Directions

Take slow cooker and melt processed cheese in it, stirring occasionally.
Take out beef, mix in taco seasoning and water and cook for about 4 minutes.
Take skillet and cook ground beef in it until brown.
Add salsa and seasoned beef into melted cheese and cook until blended.
Serve hot.

Famous meatballs

Ingredients
- Pineapple chunks in juice (1 can or 13.25 ounce)
- Soy sauce (2 tbsp)
- 1 green bell pepper, sliced
- Lemon juice (2 tbsp)
- Brown sugar (½ cup)
- Frozen cooked meatballs (1 bag or 3 pound), thawed

- **Cornstarch (2 tbsp)**

Directions

Take skillet and add pineapple chunks with juice.

Put in lemon juice through pineapple chunks, soy sauce, cornstarch, brown sugar and green bell pepper until cornstarch and sugar dissolve.

Boil and cook the above mixture for about 10 minutes, stir time to time until thickened.

Take slow cooker, put meatballs and pour the above dressing over it.

Cook for about 120 minutes, stirring occasionally and then serve.

Slow-Cooker Easy Chicken Alfredo

Ingredients for 4 servings

- Boneless, skinless chicken thighs – 1 lb. cut into ¾-inch pieces
- Sliced mushrooms – 1 (4.5-oz.) jar, drained
- Roasted red bell pepper strips – 1/3 cup, from a jar
- Dry sherry – 2 tablespoons
- Alfredo sauce – 1 (16-oz.) jar
- Frozen broccoli cuts – 3 cups

Mix and freeze in the bag

Method

1. Cook on low setting for 5 to 6 hours.
2. Meanwhile, cook fettuccine according to package instructions. Drain.
3. Stir cooked fettuccine into the chicken mixture, just before serving.
4. Sprinkle with Parmesan cheese and serve.

Nutrition Information Per Serving

- Calories 745
- Fat 43g
- Carbohydrate 51g
- Protein 44g

Slow Cooker Spaghetti and Meatballs

Ingredients for 6 servings

- Seasoned bread crumbs – ½ cup
- Romano cheese bread – 1 tablespoons
- Pepper – ½ teaspoon
- Salt – ¼ teaspoon
- Ground beef – 2 pounds
- Bay leaf – 3pc

Method

1. Gently mix the ingredients well. Then with your hands, shape into 1-1/2-inch balls.
2. Freeze all in the bag.
3. In a 6-qt. slow cooker, add your sauce ingredients. Stir in garlic and add seasonings.
4. Add meatballs to the mixture, stir to coat.
5. Cook, covered on low until meatballs are cooked through, about 5 to 6 hours.
6. Remove the bay leaves before serving. Serve with spaghetti.

Nutrition Information 1 cup (calculated without spaghetti)

- Calories 254
- Fat 11g
- Carbohydrate 20g
- Protein 20g

Slow Cooker Pot Roast

Ingredients for 6 servings

- Condensed cream of mushroom soup – 1 can (10.75 ounces)
- Dry onion soup mix – ½ can
- Pot roast – 2 ½ pounds

Mix and freeze in the bag

Method

1. In the slow cooker, add pot roast and other ingredients.
2. Cook on low setting for 8 to 9 hours or on high setting for 3 to 4 hours.

Nutrition Information Per Serving

- Calories 426
- Fat 23.7g
- Carbohydrate 4.9g
- Protein 45.6g

Slow Cooker Chicken Taco Soup

Ingredients for 4 servings

- Chili beans – 1 (8 ounce) can
- Black beans – 1 (8ounce) can
- Whole kernel corn – 1 (8ounce) can, drained
- Tomato sauce – 1 (4 ounce) can
- Diced tomatoes with green chilies – 1 (10 ounce) can, undrained
- Taco seasoning – 1 (1 ounce) package
- Skinless, boneless chicken breasts – 2 whole

Mix and freeze in the bag

Method

1. In a slow cooker, cook on low heat for 5 hours.
2. Remove chicken breasts from the soup. Let them cool so you can touch them with your hands.
3. Shred the chicken and add back into the soup.
4. Cook 2 hours more.

5. Serve topped with sour cream, shredded Cheddar cheese and crushed tortilla chips.

Nutrition Information Per Serving

- Calories 434
- Fat 17.7g
- Carbohydrate 42.3g
- Protein 27.2g

Slow Cooker Chicken and Dumplings

Ingredients for 4 servings

- Skinless, boneless chicken breast halves – 2
- Butter – 1 tablespoon
- Condensed cream chicken soup – 1 (10.75 ounces) can
- Onion – 1, finely diced

Mix and freeze in the bag

Method

1. In a slow cooker, place frozen ingredients. Add water to cover the mixture.
2. Cover, and cook on high for 5 to 6 hours.
3. Add the biscuit dough in the slow cooker about 30 minutes before serving.
4. Cook until the dough is cooked and not raw in the center.

Nutrition Information Per Serving

- Calories 385

- Fat 18g
- Carbohydrate 37g
- Protein 18.1g

Slow Cooker Italian Beef for Sandwiches

Ingredients for 4 servings

- Dried parsley – ½ teaspoon
- Garlic powder – ½ teaspoon
- Salt – ½ teaspoon
- Ground black pepper – ½ teaspoon
- Dried oregano – ½ teaspoon
- Dried basil – ½ teaspoon
- Onion salt – ½ teaspoon
- Bay leaf – 1
- Rump roast – 1 (2.5 pound)

Mix and freeze in the bag

Method

1. In the slow cooker, add the roast and the other ingredients.
2. Cover and cook on high for 4 to 5 hours, or low for 10 to 12 hours.

3. When done, shred meat with a fork, remove bay leaf and serve.

Nutrition Information Per Serving

- Calories 318
- Fat 15.8g
- Carbohydrate 1.6g
- Protein 39.4g

Slow Cooker Mexican Style Meat

Ingredients for 6 servings

- Chuck roast – 1 (2 pound)
- Salt – ½ teaspoon
- Ground black pepper – ½ teaspoon
- Olive oil – 1 tablespoon
- Onion – ½ large, chopped
- Green Chile pepper – ½ cup
- Chili powder -1/2 teaspoon
- Ground cayenne pepper – ½ teaspoon
- Hot pepper sauce – 2.5 ounce
- Garlic powder – ½ teaspoon

Mix and freeze in the bag

Method

1. In a slow cooker, place the ingredients, cover and cook for 6 hours. From time to time check to make sure there is a little amount of water in the bottom.

2. Lower heat to low and continue to cook until meat is tender and falls apart, about 2 to 4 hours.

3. Shred with fork and serve in burritos or tacos.

Nutrition Information Per Serving

- Calories 260

- Fat 19.1g

- Carbohydrate 3.3g

- Protein 18.4g

Slow Cooker Chicken Barbecue

Ingredients for 6 servings

- Skinless, boneless chicken breast halves – 6
- Italian salad dressing – ½ cup
- Brown sugar – ¼ cup
- Worcestershire sauce – 2 tablespoons

Mix and freeze in the bag

Method

1. Place the ingredients in a slow cooker. Add 12 ounces of barbecue sauce.
2. Cover and cook 6 to 8 hours on low or 3 to 4 hours on high.
3. Serve with buns.

Nutrition Information Per Serving

- Calories 300
- Fat 8.1g
- Carbohydrate 32.4g
- Protein 23g

Slow Cooker Ribs

Ingredients for 4 servings

- Meaty pork ribs – 3lb
- Pork stock cubes – 2
- Bay leaf – 2
- Coriander seed – 1 teaspoon
- Mustard seed – 1 teaspoon
- Peppercorn – 1 teaspoon

Mix and freeze in the bag

Method

1. Place all the ingredients in a slow cooker, pour 11 ounces of barbecue sauce and cook on low until very tender, about 8 to 9 hours.
2. Serve with bread.

Nutrition Information Per Serving

- Calories 414
- Fat 24.1g

- Carbohydrate 24.7g
- Protein 23.16g

Slow Cooker Rabbit Stew

Ingredients for 4 servings

- Prune – 5 oz
- Soft brown sugar – 1,7 oz
- Rabbit – 2pc, sliced
- Rashers smoked streaky bacon – 3 sliced into thin strips
- Carrots – 2, chopped
- Onion – 1, chopped
- Celery sticks – 2, chopped
- Garlic – 1 clove, crushed
- Thyme sprigs – 2
- Bay leaf – 1

Mix and freeze in the bag

Method

1. In a slow cooker, add the ingredients and pour 150 ml red wine, brandy 50 ml, 250 ml chicken stock and cook on low for 2 hours or until the rabbits are cooked.

2. Garnish with parsley and serve with wild rice.

Nutrition Information Per Serving

- Calories 450
- Fat 21g
- Carbohydrate 36g
- Protein 61g

Slow Cooker Beef Shank

Ingredients for 4 servings

- Beef crosscut shank – 2 to 2 ½ pounds, fat trimmed away
- Salt and black pepper according to taste
- Garlic -10 to 12 cloves, chopped
- Yellow onions – 2, chopped
- Celery – 1 large stalk, chopped
- Bay leaf – 1

Mix and freeze in the bag

Method

1. Add the ingredients to the slow cooker. Add 750 ml red wine, beef broth 4 cups, balsamic vinegar and vegetable oil as needed.
2. Cover and cook on low for 6 to 8 hours or until the meat extremely tender and has fallen away from the bone.
3. Serve over polenta or pasta.

Nutrition Information Per Serving

- Calories 562
- Fat 12.6g
- Carbohydrate 18.3g
- Protein 61.4g

Slow Cooker Chicken Tortilla Soup

Ingredients for 4 servings

- Shredded, cooked chicken – ½ pound
- Whole peeled tomatoes – 1 (8 ounce) can, mashed
- Onion – 1 medium, chopped
- Green chile peppers – ½ (4 ounce) can
- Garlic – 1 clove, minced
- Cumin – 1 teaspoon
- Chili powder – ½ teaspoon
- Salt – ½ teaspoon
- Black pepper – 1/8 teaspoon
- Bay leaf -1
- Frozen corn – 1(5 ounce) can

Mix and freeze in the bag

Method

1. Place ingredients in a slow cooker. Add Enchilada sauce – 1 (8 ounce) can, chicken broth – 1 (8 ounce) can, 2 cups of water and vegetable oil as needed.

2. Cover and cook on low for 6 to 8 hours or high for 3 to 4 hours.

3. Warm up 4 tortillas in a microwave oven. Cut tortillas into strips.

4. Sprinkle tortilla strips over soup and serve.

Nutrition Information Per Serving

- Calories 262
- Fat 10.6g
- Carbohydrate 24.7g
- Protein 18g

Slow Cooker Salisbury Steak

Ingredients for 4 servings

- Lean ground beef – 1 pound
- Dry onion soup mix – 1 (1 ounce) envelope
- Italian seasoned bread crumbs – ¼ cup
- Milk – 2 tablespoons
- All purpose flour – 2 tablespoons
- Dry au jus mix – 1 (1 ounce) packet

Method

1. Mix in a large bowl and shape into 4 patties.
2. Freeze in the bag.
3. Take out from the bag, dredge with flour to coat.
4. In a hot skillet, brown on both sides with vegetable oil.
5. In a slow cooker, add the patties, pour condensed cream of chicken soup 1 (10.5 ounces) can. Add water to cover.
6. Cook until ground beef is well done, about 4 to 5 hours on low heat.

7. Serve over mashed potatoes.

Nutrition Information Per Serving

- Calories 388
- Fat 24g
- Carbohydrate 18g
- Protein 23.5g

Slow-Cooker Chicken Burrito Bowls

Ingredients for 6 servings

- Boneless, skinless chicken breasts, or thighs – 1 pound
- Diced tomatoes – 1 (14.5 ounce) can
- Chili powder – 2 teaspoons
- Salt – 2 teaspoons
- Cumin – 1 teaspoon
- Black beans – 1 (15- ounce) can, drained and rinsed
- Frozen corn – 1 cup

Mix and freeze in the bag

Method

1. Add the ingredients to a slow cooker. Add chicken stock 1 cup, and water to cover the chicken. Cover and cook on low for 5 to 6 hours or until chicken is done and beans and cooked.
2. Serve over brown rice.

Nutrition Information Per Serving

- Calories 343
- Fat 4.7g
- Carbohydrate 44.8g
- Protein 30.4g

Slow-Cooker Enchilada Meatballs

Ingredients for 4 servings

- Shredded Mexican cheese blend – 20 oz.
- Crumbled cornbread – 3 cups
- Fresh cilantro – 1 cup, chopped
- Onion – 1 cup, finely chopped
- Taco seasoning mix – ¼ cup
- Garlic – 4 cloves, chopped
- Eggs – 4, slightly beaten
- Ground beef – 3lb

Method

1. Mix and make 1-inch balls with the mixture.
2. Freeze in the bag.
3. Place in a slow cooker. Add mild Enchilada sauce – 4 (10 oz.) cans. Stir to coat.
4. Cover and cook on low heat for 3 hours.
5. Sprinkle with cheese and serve.

Nutrition Information Per Ball

- Calories 60
- Fat 3.5g
- Carbohydrate 2g
- Protein 5g

Conclusion

Enjoy mouthwatering easy freeze-ahead recipes of this cookbook, eat healthy and spend more time with your family.

Part 2

Introduction

Are you convinced the Western diet is a leading contributor to or cause of chronic illnesses such as obesity, heart disease, and cancer? Want to increase energy, reduce inflammation, stabilize blood sugar, improve workouts, increase energy, help with weight loss, and possibly reduce the risk of future chronic diseases? If so, check out the delicious paleo-crockpot recipes in Paleo-Crockpot; 50 Great Recipes.

Delicious soups, stews, breakfasts, lunches, and brunches for every stage of the paleo diet! Scrumptious vegetarian meals easily tailored to your specific health goals, dietary issues, and concerns. Paleo-Crockpot; 50 Great Recipes will help you stay true to your diet and become the person you dream of!

Dieting does not have to be hard, impossible, or lead you to hate yourself. Eat healthily and feel great without being inconvenienced! Take some of the stress out of dieting, let a crockpot do most of the work. Put it in and walk away, Paleo-Crockpot; 50 Great Recipes will guide you through the process!

Paleo Egg and Nut Bread

Chopped broccoli or cauliflower are just a few possibilities in this 'bread'! Makes 1 loaf.

Ingredients:

- 2 teaspoons oil
- 4-6 large eggs
- 1 cup spinach
- 1 teaspoon sunflower seeds
- 1 teaspoon celery salt
- 1 teaspoon paprika
- 1 teaspoon turmeric

Directions:
1. Coat bottom of crockpot with oil.
2. Add eggs and scramble for 30 seconds.
3. Add the spinach, sunflower seeds, celery salt, paprika, and if using it turmeric and mix well.
4. Cook on high 45 minutes to 1 hour depending upon how 'stiff' you desire it.

Honey Glazed Shrimp

Scallops work too! Makes 4 servings

Ingredients:

- 2-3 cups broccoli and cauliflower
- 1 bell peppers sliced
- 1 onion diced
- 1 Tbsp slivered almonds
- 1 tablespoon honey
- 1 teaspoon (dried or fresh) thyme
- 4 cups water or chicken stock
- 1-pound large shrimp, cleaned and deveined

Directions:
1. In small bowl mix almonds and honey together then set aside.
2. Place in broccoli and cauliflower, bell pepper slices, and onion.
3. Top with honey nuts and sprinkle with thyme.
4. Add uncooked shrimp and pour in liquid.

5. Cook on low 45 minutes to 1 hour.

Squash Bake

Perfect for fresh herbs! Makes 4 servings.
Ingredients:

- 1 large spaghetti squash
- ¼ cup diced onion
- 1 cup halved cherry tomatoes
- 1 teaspoon minced garlic
- 1 teaspoon Italian oregano, diced
- 1 teaspoon parsley flakes
- 2 cups water or chicken stock

Directions:
1. Preheat oven to 350 and bake squash for 1 hour. To avoid a buildup of steam put holes in the sides of squash. When done cooking remove and let cool completely.
2. With fork shred squash and place in large mixing bowl with onion, tomatoes, garlic, basil, and parsley. Mix ingredients together.

3. Put mixture into crockpot along with 2 cups of water.
4. Cook on high 45 minutes to 1 hour.

Almond Honey Chicken Dippers

Great for little kids, big kids, and quick healthy lunches! Makes 4 servings.

Ingredients:

- 3 Tbsp olive oil
- 4 boneless, skinless chicken breasts
- 2 cups almond flower
- 1 teaspoon Beau Monde seasoning (onion powder, garlic powder, and celery flakes
- 2 eggs
- 2 cups honey
- 1 cup diced broccoli

Directions:
Use two bowls (a & b)
1. In bowl a beat the eggs and in bowl b combine the almond flour and celery flakes

2. Dredge each chicken breast and coat in egg then in flour mixture.
3. Place into the bottom of crockpot coated with olive oil.
4. Add broccoli.
5. Drizzle honey over chicken and broccoli
6. Cook on low 1-1 hour twenty minutes.

Paleo Pineapple & Walnut Applesauce

For a fall treat add 2 teaspoons of cinnamon and 1/2 tsp of nutmeg! Makes 4 servings.

Ingredients:

- 2 red apples cut into 1-inch pieces
- 2 green apples cut into 1-inch pieces
- 1 cup walnuts
- 3/4 cup honey
- 3 tablespoons pineapple juice

Directions:
1. Prepare apples and put into crockpot.
2. Add walnuts.
3. Pour honey over the fruit and nut pieces.
4. Add pineapple juice.
5. Cook on low 30-45 minutes hours.

Cinnamon Pumpkin Soup

Great for those busy autumn nights! Makes 2 servings.

Ingredients:

- Olive oil
- 2 cans pumpkin
- 2 cup diced cauliflower
- ½ cup coconut milk
- 2 teaspoons cinnamon

Directions:

1. In a food processor puree cauliflower.
2. Add pumpkin, cauliflower puree, coconut milk and cinnamon to crockpot.
3. Cook on low 45 minutes to 1 hour.

Paleo Sweet & Sour Cabbage

Try it with ground pork! Makes 4 servings.
Ingredients:

- 2 cups sweet and sour sauce, see recipe below
- 4 cups purple cabbage
- 1/3 cup chicken stock or water
- ¼ cup diced scallions
- 2 teaspoons minced or ground ginger
- 1 tablespoon grated carrots
- Sweet and Sour Sauce
- 1 cup pineapple juice
- 1 tablespoon raw honey
- 2 teaspoon red pepper flakes
- 1/4 teaspoon ginger

Directions:
1. Prepare sauce and cabbage

2. Put both along with water, scallions, ginger, and carrots into crockpot and stir well.
3. Cook on high 2-4 hours.

Immune Boosting Chicken Soup

Dark meat as it is higher in zinc! Makes 4 servings.
Ingredients:
- 4 cups chicken stock or vegetable stock
- 4 cups shredded chicken
- 1/2 cup spinach or kale
- ¼ cup matchstick carrots
- ½ Tbsp minced garlic
- 1/2 tablespoon minced ginger
- 1/2 tablespoon diced thyme
- ½ Tbsp diced oregano
- 1 Tbsp diced parsley
- 1 teaspoons turmeric

Directions:

1. To crockpot add shredded chicken, spinach/kale, carrots, garlic, ginger, thyme, oregano, parsley, turmeric.

2. Cook on low 30 minutes to 1 hour.

Paleo Brownies

For coconut flavor add in some coconut oil! Makes 8-11 brownies

Ingredients:

- 1 ½ cups almond flour
- 1 cup unsweetened cocoa powder
- 1 teaspoon baking soda
- ½ teaspoon baking powder
- ½ cup strong coffee or espresso
- 2 egg yolks
- 1 egg white
- If desired 1 tablespoon of sugar substitute or raw honey

Directions:

1. Add flour, cocoa powder, baking soda, baking powder, espresso, egg yolks, and egg whites to crockpot and stir well.

2. Cook on low ½ to 1 hour.

Squash, Broccoli, and Cauliflower Bake

So good you'll forget it is good for you! Makes 4 servings

Ingredients:

- 1 Tbsp olive oil
- 1 acorn or butternut squash cut inti 2 x 2 pieces
- 1 cup diced broccoli pieces, roughly 1 x 1
- 1 cup diced cauliflower pieces, roughly 1 x 1
- Crushed walnuts or pinenuts (optional)
- ½ tsp minced garlic
- 1 tsp minced onion
- Black pepper to taste
- 1 tablespoon lemon juice
- 1 teaspoon thyme

Directions:

1. Pour 1 tablespoon of olive oil into bottom of crockpot.
2. Place squash, broccoli, cauliflower, walnuts, garlic, onions, black pepper, lemon juice, thyme.
3. Cook 45 minutes to 1 hour on high.

Spicy Sausage, Basil and Eggs

Great meal for a late breakfast or weekend brunch! Makes 2 servings

Ingredients:

- Vegan sausage
- 4 eggs, scrambled
- 1 tablespoon ghee or organic clarified butter
- 1/3 cup basil leaves
- 2 teaspoons black pepper
- 2 teaspoons red pepper flakes
- 1 cup spinach or kale

Directions:
1. Put eggs, butter, and basil, black pepper, and red pepper flakes into crockpot and stir well.
2. Empty package of sausage into egg mixture and pour spinach or kale in also. Stir together.
3. Cook 45 minutes to 30-45 minutes on high.

Spiced Chicken Kabobs on a Bed of Cabbage

Cauliflower, broccoli, spinach, or kale are just a few possible great substitutions for the cabbage. Makes 4 servings.

Ingredients:

- 4-6 skewers
- Coconut oil
- 1/2 lbs. boneless skinless chicken breasts, cut into cubes roughly 2 x 2
- 1 head of cabbage, chopped
- 1 medium onion, diced
- ½ tsp garlic, minced
- 1 teaspoon turmeric
- 1/3 cup water
- 1 cup honey
- 2 tablespoons molasses
- 1 tablespoon chili powder
- 1 teaspoon cumin

Directions:

1. In a large mixing bowl stir together the honey, molasses, chili powder, and cumin.
2. Cut chicken into bite sized cubes and thread on skewers that have been soaked 30 minutes in cold water.
3. Pour sauce over skewers coating each piece.
4. Place chucks of cabbage into food processor. When cabbage reduced to rice sized pieces place into crockpot.
5. Pour in onion, garlic, turmeric, and water. Stir well
6. Top cabbage with marinated chicken.
7. Cook on high 1-2 hours.

Never eat under cooked chicken! If meat is pink or runs unclear juices continue cooking. CDC states chicken is done when 165 degrees.

Fiery Beef, Asparagus, and Brussel Sprouts

Instead of jalapenos try habaneros or ghost peppers!
Makes 4 servings
Ingredients:

- 1 Tbsp olive oil
- ¼ lbs. beef strips
- 2 jalapeno peppers, chopped and seeded
- 1 teaspoon garlic minced
- 1/2 cup white vinegar
- 1/3 cup honey
- 1 teaspoon cayenne pepper
- 1 diced red bell pepper
- 2 teaspoon celery salt
- 2 cups asparagus spears
- 2 cups brussel sprout

Directions:
1. In a food processor put jalapeno peppers, garlic, vinegar, honey, and cayenne pepper. Puree.

2. Place asparagus spears, Brussel sprouts, diced red pepper, and celery salt in crockpot.
3. Put beef into pot and cover with jalapeno puree. Stir well.
4. Cook on high 45 minutes-1 hour.

Squash and Sausage in Mushroom Gravy

Delicious! Makes 4 servings.
Ingredients:

- 1 Butternut squash, cubed approx. 1 x 1
- 1/3 andouille sausage
- 2 cubes beef bouillon cubes
- 1/3 cup water
- 1 tablespoon Worcester sauce
- 1 cup finely diced white or button mushrooms
- 1 teaspoon black pepper
- 2 teaspoons thyme

Directions:
1. Place butternut squash, sausage pieces, bullion, water, Worcester sauce, mushrooms, black pepper, and thyme; mix well and bring to boil.
2. Cook on high 45 minutes to 1 hour.

Paleo Jambalaya

Great with or without protein! Makes 4 servings.
Ingredients:

- 2 cubes beef bullion
- 2 cups water
- 1 (8 oz) can no salt tomato sauce
- 1/3 cup chopped celery
- 1 (14 oz) can no salt diced tomatoes
- 1 tablespoon lemon juice
- ¼ teaspoon orange peel
- ½ teaspoon black pepper
- 1 red bell peppers chopped
- 2 teaspoons dried basil
- 2 cups scallops
- 1 lbs. medium shrimp
- 2 diced fillets of cod or wild salmon

- 1 cup clams

Directions:
1. Whisk together bullion and water.
2. Put in crockpot tomatoes, tomato sauce, celery, lemon juice, orange peel, black pepper, and roast bell peppers.
3. Place all proteins into crockpot.
4. Cook on high 1-3 hours.

Paleo Spinach and Kale

Canned, frozen, or fresh vegetables work equally well in this recipe! Makes 4 servings.

Ingredients:

- 2 cups water
- 1 teaspoon apple cider vinegar
- Juice of ½ lemon
- 1 tablespoon finely diced onion
- 2 cups spinach
- 2 cups kale
- 1 teaspoon turmeric

Directions:

1. In crockpot put bouillon cubes, water, Worcester sauce, and lemon juice.
2. Add onions, spinach, kale, and turmeric.
3. Cook on low 1-2 hours.

Pearl Onions and Spinach

Make good meals! Makes 2 servings.
Ingredients:

- 3 vegetable bouillon cubes
- 1 Tbsp no salt tomato sauce
- 1 cup spinach
- 1 cup pearl onions
- 1 teaspoon oregano
- 1 teaspoon thyme
- 1 teaspoon parsley
- 3 basil leaves or 1 teaspoon dried basil
- 1 teaspoon sage
- 1 teaspoon rosemary

Directions:
1. Add water, bouillon cubes, tomato sauce, spinach, pearl onions. Stir well.

2. Add oregano, thyme, parsley, basil, sage, and rosemary. Stir well.

3. Cook 2-3 hours on low.

Paleo Crockpot Sweet Onions

For added kick throw in some peppers! Makes 5-8 servings

Ingredients:

- Olive oil
- ½ teaspoon thyme
- 2 cups chicken, beef, or vegetarian stock
- 2 sweet onions, sliced

Directions:

1. Place beef, olive oil, thyme, stock, and onions in crockpot.
2. Cook 1-2 hours on low.

Paleo Bacon Bake

Any type of bacon can work too! Makes 2-4 servings.
Ingredients:

- 4 cups chicken or vegetable stock
- 4 strips of turkey bacon, cut into fine pieces approx.1 cm x 1 cm
- ½ cup squash
- 1 cup chopped chunks of carrot
- 1 sweet onion, sliced
- 1 cup diced broccoli
- 1 cup diced cauliflower
- 1 teaspoon diced fresh oregano or dried
- 1 teaspoon black pepper

Directions:
1. Prepare turkey pieces.
2. Add squash, carrot, onions, broccoli, cauliflower, oregano, and pepper; mix well.

3. Pour stock into crockpot.
4. Cook on high 30-45 minutes.

Eggplant & Ham Ragu

Sub cabbage for the eggplant! Makes 4-6 servings.

Ingredients:

- 1 large eggplant, chopped
- 1 cup small cubed ham
- 1 tablespoon olive oil
- ½ diced shallot
- 2 teaspoons garlic, minced
- 1 diced celery stalk
- 1 8 oz. can no salt tomato sauce
- 6 cups tomato diced
- 1-2 cups raw honey

Directions:

1. In bottom of pot sauté the shallot, garlic, and celery over olive oil 30 seconds
2. Pour in ham cubes and sauté into onion mix, 30 seconds.
3. Pour in tomato sauce, diced tomatoes, and honey, stirring constantly. Continue this for 30-45 seconds.

4. Add in eggplant and top with meat mixture. Continue this pattern until all ingredients is gone or a sufficient height is reached.
5. Cook 1-2 hours on low.

Chicken & Ginger Casserole

An easy paleo dish that is great! Makes 4 servings.
Ingredients:

- 1 tablespoon olive oil or coconut oil
- 1 tablespoon arrowroot starch
- 1/3 cup white vinegar
- 2 cups shredded chicken
- 1/3 diced green onions
- 1 tablespoon grated carrots
- 1 tablespoon minced or grated ginger
- 1 teaspoon cumin

Directions:
1. Place oil, starch, wine, chicken, onions, carrots, ginger, and cumin.
2. Cook 30-45 minutes on high.

Apple & Cinnamon Stuffed Peppers

For easy clean-up marinate the meat in a sealed plastic bag! Makes 4 servings.

Ingredients:

- 4 multi-colored bell pepper
- 1 small pork tenderloin
- 1 tablespoon olive or coconut oil, divided
- 1 tablespoon apple cider vinegar
- 1 teaspoon cinnamon
- 1 teaspoon garlic powder
- 1 teaspoon pepper
- Non-stick spray
- 1/3 cup water or stock

Directions:
1. Marinade pork in a large plastic bag with oil, apple cider vinegar, cinnamon, garlic powder, pepper.
2. Brown pork in a skillet 1-3 minutes per side depending on weight.

3. Cut the top off peppers, remove seeds and ribs, then wash out.
4. Spray crockpot.
5. Fill peppers with meat in, lay in crockpot, pour in stock.
6. Cook on high 45 minutes to 1 hour.

Cauliflower Stuffed Peppers

A paleo-vegan take on this classic comfort food! Makes 4 servings

Ingredients:

- 4 bell peppers, tops cut off, seeds and ribs removed
- 2 teaspoons olive oil or coconut oil
- 1 ½ cups cauliflower, chopped or grated to rice size
- 1/2 tablespoon diced onions
- ½ tablespoon celery
- 4-6 oz. tomato sauce
- 1 teaspoon thyme
- 1 teaspoon oregano
- 1 teaspoon garlic powder
- 1/3 cup beef stock or water

Directions:

1. In bottom of crockpot sauté onions and celery 1 minute.
2. Add cauliflower, tomato sauce, thyme, oregano, and garlic powder; mix well. Let cool.

3. Fill peppers with mix, place in crockpot.
4. Pour liquid around peppers and cook 30-45 minutes on high.

Zucchini Lasagna

Equally delicious with zucchini noodles! Makes 4 servings.

Ingredients:

- 2 large zucchinis cut in thin lengthwise strips
- 1 tablespoon olive oil or coconut oil
- 1/2 tablespoon minced garlic
- 1 diced tablespoon sweet onion
- 1 8 oz. can no salt tomato sauce
- 2 teaspoon basil
- 2 teaspoon parsley
- ½ cup diced mushrooms
- 1/3 cup matchstick carrot

Directions:
1. Pour oil into crockpot and swirl covering bottom.
2. Cover bottom with layer of zucchini strips.

3. Combine garlic, onion, tomato sauce, basil, parsley, mushrooms, carrots.
4. Spread thin layer across zucchini strips.
5. Repeat
6. Cook 30-45 minutes on high.

Veggie Ragu

Change it up with different proteins. Makes 1 serving.
Ingredients:

- 2 tablespoons olive or coconut oil
- Vegetable noodles (ex-zucchini, cucumber, carrot, summer squash)
- 2/3-1 cup chicken stock or water
- 1/3 cup diced tomatoes
- 5-6 pearl onions
- 1 tablespoon diced black olives
- ½ tsp Greek seasoning

Directions:
1. Pour oil into crockpot
2. Add in noodles and stock.
3. Add tomatoes, onions, olives, and Greek seasoning
4. Cook 45 minutes to 1 hour on high.

Squash Chili

A great dish for a fall day in! Makes 4 servings.

Ingredients:

- 3 1/2 cups organic vegetable stock
- 1/2 cups water
- 1/3 cup cornstarch
- 1 teaspoon cinnamon
- 1/3 diced asparagus
- 1 cup finely diced eggplant
- 1 cup cubed butternut or acorn squash
- ¼ cup pumpkin seeds
- 1 teaspoon honey
- ½ teaspoon paprika

Directions:

1. Pour into crockpot stock, water, starch, and cinnamon.
2. Add asparagus, eggplant, squash, and pumpkin seeds.
3. Cook 1-2 hours on high.

Zesty Turkey Chili

For added heat, add jalapeno powder! Makes 4 servings.

Ingredients:

- I lbs. organic ground turkey
- 3 tablespoons olive oil or coconut oil
- 1 diced sweet onion
- 1 tablespoon minced garlic
- 1 diced celery stalk
- 2 finely diced habaneros
- 3 teaspoons chili powder
- 3 teaspoons paprika
- 2 teaspoons turmeric
- 1 teaspoon cumin
- 3-4 cups water

Directions:

1. In crockpot put oil, onion, garlic, celery, habaneros, chili powder, turmeric, paprika, cumin and water.
2. Cook on high 30-45 minutes.

Curried Collards

Mustard greens work too! Makes 4 servings.
Ingredients:

- 3 cups collard greens
- 2 cups water or stock
- 1 teaspoon garlic pepper
- 1 teaspoon black pepper
- 2 teaspoons turmeric
- 1 diced bell pepper
- 1 tsp curry powder

Directions:
1. Add garlic pepper, black pepper, turmeric, bell pepper, and curry powder.
2. Pour in collards and liquid.
3. Cook 30-45 minutes on high.

Noodles Soup

Great over cauliflower rice! Makes 4 servings.

Ingredients:

- 1 tablespoon olive oil
- 1 cup diced tomatoes
- 1/4 cup no salt tomato sauce
- 1 diced shallot
- 1 teaspoon garlic powder
- I teaspoon basil diced fresh
- 1 teaspoon oregano diced fresh or dried
- 1 teaspoon thyme fresh or dried
- 1 cup browned and drained ground beef

Directions:

1. Pour olive oil, tomatoes, tomato sauce, shallot, garlic.
2. Add basil, oregano, thyme, and protein.
3. Cook 30-45 minutes on high.

Squash Casserole

Any seasonal squash will work! Makes 4 servings.
Ingredients:

- 1 cup shredded squash
- 1 bell pepper, chopped
- 4 plum tomatoes, quartered
- 2 oz. tomato paste
- ¼ cup water or chicken stock
- 1/3 teaspoon lemon peel
- 1/3 teaspoon sea salt
- 1/3 teaspoon garlic powder
- 1/3 teaspoon black or white pepper

Directions:
1. In large bowl mix squash, peppers, and tomatoes.
2. Mix in tomato paste, water, sea salt, garlic powder, pepper.
3. Cook on low 30-45 minutes.

Okra Soup

Delicious! Makes 4 servings.
Ingredients:

- 1/3 tablespoon olive or coconut oil
- 1/4 cup petite diced tomatoes
- 1 container no salt beef stock
- 2 teaspoons tapioca starch
- 1 tablespoon julienned onion
- 1 teaspoon garlic powder
- 1 teaspoon cinnamon
- 3 cups okra

Directions:
1. Pour tomatoes, tapioca starch, onion, garlic powder, cinnamon, okra and stock into crockpot. Stir well.
2. Cook on high 4 hours.

Spicy Cabbage and Onions

Sub lettuce for cabbage! Makes 4 servings.

Ingredients:

- 3 tablespoons olive oil or coconut oil
- 2 cups grated cabbage
- 1/2 cups julienned onions
- 1/3 cup walnuts or slivered almonds
- 1 teaspoon cornstarch
- 1/4 cup white wine
- 1 teaspoon red pepper flakes
- ½ cup chicken stock

Directions:
1. In crockpot place the cabbage, onions, nuts, cornstarch, white wine, red pepper flakes, and stock.
2. Stir well.
3. Cook on high 3-5 hours.

Caramelized Onions

These onions make great additions to sauces, sandwiches, and burgers! Makes ¾-1 cups.

Ingredients:

- 1 cup onion sliced
- 1 stick butter or ½ cup olive oil
- 1 teaspoon pepper
- 1 Tbsp brown sugar
- 1/3 Tbsp Worchester sauce

Directions:

1. Place in crockpot butter/oil, onions, pepper, brown sugar, Worchester sauce.
2. Cook 8-10 hours on low.

Fall Spice Applesauce

Allspice works too! Makes 4-8 servings

Ingredients:

- 10 organic apples, washed, cored, and sliced
- 1/2 stick butter
- 1 tablespoon organic honey
- 1 tablespoon lemon juice
- 1/3 tablespoon cinnamon
- 1/4 teaspoon nutmeg or cloves

Directions:
1. Prepare apples and put into crockpot.
2. Add butter or oil, lemon juice, cinnamon, nutmeg.
3. Cook on low 5-6 hours stirring occasionally.

Grilled Salmon and Pomegranate Mint Applesauce

Works with any lean protein! Makes 2-4 serving.
Ingredients:

- 1 1/2 cups pomegranate, washed
- 4 cups sliced and cored organic apples
- ½ stick butter
- ½ cup water
- 1/2 teaspoon lemon juice
- 1 tablespoon organic honey
- 1 tablespoon diced mint
- 2-4 fillets of wild caught salmon

Directions:
1. Put apples, pomegranate, butter, lemon juice, honey and mint into crockpot and stir.
2. Cook on low 4-6 hours.
3. Cook filets over medium high heat 45 seconds -1 minute per side.

For a quick paleo marinade try ½ cup olive oil, 1 tsp minced garlic, 1 Tbsp honey, ½ Tbsp lemon juice, 1/3 tsp pepper. Let filets marinate in fridge 10-15 minutes.

Cauliflower Rice & Chicken Casserole

Try it with different proteins. Makes 4 servings.

Ingredients:

- 2 Tbsp olive oil
- 1 cup shredded chicken
- 2 cups thyme
- 1 diced shallot
- 1 diced carrot
- 1 cup broccoli florets
- 3 cups cauliflower rice
- 2 teaspoons diced mint fresh or dried
- 4 cups chicken stock or water

Directions:

1. Combine oil, chicken, thyme, shallot, carrots, broccoli, cauliflower, mint, liquid.
2. Cook 30-55 minutes on low.

Zucchini Noodle Slow Cooker Mac and Cheese

Great with or without bacon! Makes 4-6 servings.
Ingredients:

- 4 cups zucchini noodles
- ¼ cup crumbled bacon
- 1 diced green onion
- 1 teaspoon dry mustard
- 1 tablespoon nutritional yeast
- 1/4 cup water
- 1 cup coconut milk
- 1 tablespoon lemon juice
- 1 teaspoon black pepper

Directions:
1. To the crockpot add zucchini noodles, dry mustard, nutritional yeast, water, coconut milk, lemon juice, and black pepper.

2. Cook bacon in skillet over medium high heat. Remove the bacon and add the diced onion to the grease and cook 1-2 minutes.
3. Add diced bacon, bacon grease and onions to the noodle mix.
4. Cook on high 4 hours.

Slow Cooker Paleo Enchiladas

2 simple steps to a delicious and filling meal! Makes 4 servings.

Ingredients:

- 1 tablespoon olive oil
- 1/2 lbs. organic ground beef, browned and drained
- 2 cups cabbage, grated or rice size
- 1 diced onion
- 1 diced bell pepper
- 1 teaspoon cayenne powder or paprika
- 2 cups diced tomatoes
- Grated parmesan cheese (optional)

Directions:

1. Pour olive oil, ground beef, cabbage, onion, bell pepper, cayenne powder or paprika, and diced tomatoes. Stir well.
2. Cook 1-1 1/2 hours on high.

Paleo Seafood Delight

Nutritious, easy, and filling! Makes 4 servings.
Ingredients:

- ½ lbs. prawns, cleaned, deveined, and de-tailed
- ½ lbs. clams
- ½ lbs. large scallops
- 1 cup clam juice
- 1 cup white wine
- 2 cups water
- 1 teaspoon lemon juice
- ½ teaspoon orange peel
- 1 teaspoon red pepper flakes
- 1 teaspoon thyme
- 3 tablespoons arrowroot or tapioca starch (optional)
- ¼ cup diced celery stalk
- 1 diced butternut squash

Directions:
1. Place prawns, clams, scallops, clam juice, white wine, water, lemon juice, orange peel, red pepper flakes, thyme, arrowroot/tapioca starch if using, celery, and butternut squash. Stir well.
2. Cook 4-6 hours on high.

Spicy Autumn Stew

A great dinner for those busy winter weeknights! Makes 4 servings.

Ingredients:

- 1 large eggplant, washed and cubed
- 1 autumn squash, washed and cubed
- 1 small pumpkin, flesh only, cubed
- 1 tablespoon pumpkin seeds
- 1 cup collard greens
- ½ tsp pepper
- ½ tsp smoked paprika
- 4 cups water
- 1/4 teaspoons turmeric
- ¼ tsp ginger

Directions:

1. Prepare foods for cooking. Put prepared eggplant, squash, pumpkin seeds, collards greens, pepper, smoked paprika, turmeric, and ginger into crockpot.
2. Pour in water and stir well.
3. Cook on high 6-8 hours.

Paleo Cucumber Pasta and Strawberries

Try different veggie spirals! Makes 4 servings.
Ingredients:

- 2 cucumbers, spiral
- 1 cup strawberries, diced, if possible, save some of the juice
- Strawberry juice
- 1 tablespoon olive oil
- 2 teaspoons water
- 1 teaspoon lemon juice
- 1 teaspoon finely diced basil (fresh or dried)
- 1 tablespoon pine nuts
- 1 cup spinach (optional)

Directions:
1. Make spiral noodles with the cucumbers.

2. Slice the strawberries saving any of the juice if possible.
3. Put the noodles, strawberries, and any of the juice into crockpot along with olive oil, water, lemon juice, basil, and nuts.
4. Cook on high 30-45 minutes.

Pumpkin Soup

Works with canned sweet potato too! Makes 4 servings.

Ingredients:

- 2 tablespoons grass fed butter
- 4 cups pumpkin
- ¼ cup pumpkin seeds
- 2 teaspoons cinnamon
- ¼ cup diced scallions
- 1 Tbsp diced black olives
- 4-6 cups beef or vegetarian stock or water

Directions:
1. Place butter, pumpkin, pumpkin seeds, spinach or scallions, and black olives in crockpot.
2. Cook 6-8 hours on high.

Paleo Crockpot Chicken Casserole

Great for gatherings! Makes 4 servings.
Ingredients:

- 1/3 cup olive oil
- 2 Tbsp butter
- 1 cup ground chicken
- 1 cup shredded cabbage
- 1 cup chunked pineapple
- ¼ cup pineapple juice
- ¼ cup chopped bok choy
- 1 cup cauliflower rice
- 1/3 cup water or red pepper and ginger broth

Directions:
1. Into crockpot place chicken, cabbage, pineapple, pineapple juice, bok choy, cauliflower rice and water; stir well.
2. Cook on low 1-2 hours.

5-Step Paleo Chicken Nugget's

Kids of all ages love them! Makes 12-15 "nuggets".
Ingredients:

- 1 boneless, skinless chicken breasts, cut in 2 x 2 pieces
- Olive oil spray
- 1/3 tsp garlic powder
- ¼ tsp onion powder
- 1/2 teaspoon paprika

Directions:
1. Prepare chicken pieces.
2. Spray crockpot.
3. Mix together garlic powder, onion powder, paprika.
4. Lay chicken pieces in single letter.
5. Sprinkle with seasoning mix and spray liberally with olive oil spray.

6. Cook on high 45 minutes to 1 hour.

Tangy Mango Sauce

A great sauce for any of your favorite meats, and you choose the right amount of 'tang' for yourself! Makes approx. 1 cup.

Ingredients:

- 1 diced mango
- 1 diced kiwi
- 1 diced onion
- 1 diced pepper (your choice of pepper)
- 3 cups molasses
- 2 cups ketchup
- 1 tablespoon dry mustard powder
- 1 teaspoon turmeric or chili powder
- 1 teaspoon garlic powder
- 1 teaspoon ginger minced or ground

Directions:
1. Place in crockpot mango, kiwi, onion, pepper, molasses, ketchup. Mustard powder, turmeric or chili powder, garlic powder, and ginger; stir well.
2. Cook on low 45 minutes.

Paleo Tacos

No tortillas need! Makes 4 servings.
Ingredients:

- 2 teaspoons grass fed butter, melted, and divided
- 1 head of lettuce leaves torn into 5x5 sections.
- 1 lbs. organic ground beef, browned and drained
- ¼ cup organic salsa
- ½ teaspoon thyme
- ½ tsp lime zest

Directions:
1. Brown hamburger in pot along with onions, salsa, thyme, lime zest.
2. Drain.
3. Layout lettuce sections fill with ground beef mixture and roll up.
4. Melt butter in crockpot and the rest into the ground beef mixture.

5. Place lettuce tacos inside crockpot.
6. Cook on low 30-45 minutes.

Salmon Salsa

Serve over rice! Makes 4 servings.
Ingredients:

- 1 tablespoon olive oil
- 4 wild caught salmon fillets
- 1/3 cup halved cherry tomatoes
- 1/3 cup diced celery
- 1/3 diced cucumber
- 1/3 cup diced eggplant
- 1/4 tsp lemon juice peel
- ¼ tsp pepper
- 1/3 tsp red pepper flakes
- 1/3 cup white wine
- 1 tsp diced oregano
- 1/2 tsp parsley

Directions:

1. Put olive oil, salmon, cherry tomatoes, diced celery, diced cucumber, diced eggplant, lemon peel, win, oregano, parsley in crockpot.
2. Cook 45 minutes to 1 hour on low.

Spinach and Mushroom in Squash Bowls

Unforgettable! Makes 4 servings.
Ingredients:

- 1 tablespoon olive oil
- 1 cup diced butternut squash
- 2/3 cups cauliflower rice
- 1 cup sliced mushrooms
- 1 teaspoon pepper
- 1 teaspoon oregano
- 2/3 tsp thyme.
- 1 teaspoon lemon peel
- 1-2 chicken stock (optional)

Directions:
1. In crockpot add oil, squash, cauliflower rice, mushroom pieces, pepper, oregano, lemon peel.
2. Cook on low 45 minutes to 1 hour.

Paleo Asparagus Ragu

Try it with sweet potatoes noodles! Makes 2-3 servings.
Ingredients:

- 2-3 cups zucchini noodles
- 1/3 cups diced asparagus
- ½ tsp minced garlic
- 1/4 cup diced, multi-colored bell peppers
- 1/3 cup diced tomatoes and juice
- 1/2 cup cubed firm silken tofu
- ½ cup browned and drained ground beef
- 4-6 cups vegetarian, beef, or chicken stock

Directions:
1. Place in crockpot zucchini noodles, asparagus, garlic, bell peppers, canned tomatoes, tofu, ground beef, stock.
2. Cook on high 30-45 minutes.

Paleo Chicken Kabobs and Kiwi Salad

Reductions in consuming dairy hurt bone health, make up for it with this delicious recipe! Makes 2 servings.

Ingredients:

- 1 boneless, skinless chicken breasts, cubed
- 4 skewers, soaked for 30 minutes in cold water
- 1/3 cup plain Greek yogurt
- 1/3 tsp Greek seasoning
- 1 diced kiwi
- 1 cup cranberries or pomegranate
- 1 tablespoon lemon juice
- 1/3 cup water
- 1 teaspoon basil
- 1 teaspoon parsley

Directions:
1. In small bowl combine yogurt and Greek seasoning.
2. Thread chicken cubes onto skewers.
3. Brush seasoned yogurt over individual chicken cubes then lay in crockpot.
4. Add in kiwi, cranberries or pomegranate, lemon juice, water, basil, parsley.
5. Cook 45 minutes on high.

IF CHICKEN IS PINK INSIDE OR RUNNING UNCLEAR JUICES CONTINUE COOKING. EATING UNDERCOOKED CHICKEN AS IT IS A HAZARD TO YOUR HEALTH. CDC RECOMMENDS COOKING TO INTERNAL TEMP OF 165.

Salsa Verde Chicken

This recipe pairs brilliantly with Spanish rice.
Serves: 6

Time: 10 min

Ingredients

- Chicken Breasts (2lbs, boneless)
- Black Beans (15oz., rinsed, and drained)
- Sweet Corn (15 oz.)
- Salsa Verde (16 oz.)

Directions

1. Add all your ingredients into a gallon sized Ziploc bag.
2. Squeeze out the excess air, seal then label your bag with the ingredients, name of the dish, directions for preparation, and date.

3. Lay flat in your freezer and freeze until you are ready to cook (lasts up to 3 months).

Balsamic Beef & Carrots

Here is a simple yet delicious dish that can be served for dinner.

Serves: 6

Time: 10 min

Ingredients

- Beef Roast (2 lbs)
- Carrots (2 jumbo, chopped)
- Balsamic Vinegar (1/2 cup)
- Soy Sauce (1/4 cup)
- Honey (2 tbsp.)
- Orange Zest (2 tsp.)
- Salt (1 tsp.)
- Black Pepper (1 tsp.)

Directions

1. Add all your ingredients into a gallon sized Ziploc bag.

2. Squeeze out the excess air, seal then label your bag with the ingredients, name of the dish, directions for preparation, and date.

3. Lay flat in your freezer and freeze until you are ready to cook (lasts up to 3 months).

Shrimp & Noodles

This recipe combines spicy and aromatic flavors that develop while frozen.

Serves: 6

Time: 10 minutes

Ingredients:

- 2lb. skinless and boneless chicken breasts, cubed
- 2 tablespoons red curry paste
- 2 tablespoons olive oil
- 8oz. dry rice noodles
- 1 lime, juiced
- 14oz. can coconut milk
- ¼ cup smooth peanut butter

- 4 tablespoons soy sauce
- ½ cup chicken stock
- 1 green bell pepper, sliced
- 4 sprigs green onions, chopped
- ¼ cup bean sprouts
- ¼ cup cilantro, chopped
- 2 tablespoons brown sugar
- 1 white onion, diced
- 6 Thai chili peppers, sliced
- 1 tablespoon minced ginger
- 1 tsp each, Salt and pepper

Directions

1. Add all your ingredients into a gallon sized Ziploc bag.

2. Squeeze out the excess air, seal then label your bag with the ingredients, name of the dish, directions for preparation, and date.

3. Lay flat in your freezer and freeze until you are ready to cook (lasts up to 3 months).

Chicken Teriyaki

A traditional dish in a bag.
Serves: 6

Time: 10 min

Ingredients

- Chicken Breasts (2lbs, boneless)
- Asian Frozen Vegetable Mix (2 packages)
- Honey (2 tbsp.)
- Soy Sauce (1/4 cup)
- Apple Cider Vinegar (2 tsp.)
- Onion (1, diced)
- Salt (1 tsp.)
- Black Pepper (1 tsp.)

Directions

1. Add all your ingredients into a gallon sized Ziploc bag.

2. Squeeze out the excess air, seal then label your bag with the ingredients, name of the dish, directions for preparation, and date.

3. Lay flat in your freezer and freeze until you are ready to cook (lasts up to 3 months).

Crockpot Curried Chicken

If you love rich and flavorful curries then but often don't have the time to prepare all the ingredients then cook, here's a recipe that should help.

Serves: 4

Time:10 minutes

Ingredients:

- 14oz. full fat coconut milk
- 1.5lb. skinless and boneless chicken breasts, diced
- 2 tablespoons red curry paste
- 2 tablespoons brown sugar
- ¼ cup peanut butter
- 3 tablespoons lime juice
- 2 tablespoons fish sauce
- ½ cup chicken stock
- ½ teaspoon red pepper flakes
- ½ teaspoon fresh minced ginger

- 4 garlic cloves, crushed

Directions

1. Add all your ingredients into a gallon sized Ziploc bag.

2. Squeeze out the excess air, seal then label your bag with the ingredients, name of the dish, directions for preparation, and date.

3. Lay flat in your freezer and freeze until you are ready to cook (lasts up to 3 months).

Spring Thyme Chicken Stew

This recipe is perfect for those cold winter nights.
Serves: 4

Time: 15 minutes

Ingredients:

- 1.5lb. 5 chicken thighs
- 1 tablespoon Worcestershire sauce
- 14oz. can coconut milk
- ½ cup chicken stock
- 2 tablespoons fish sauce
- 2 tablespoons brown sugar
- 4 tablespoon red curry paste
- 1 tablespoon lemon juice
- 2 limes, juiced and zested
- 1 tablespoon olive oil
- 1 teaspoon salt and pepper

Directions

1. Add all your ingredients into a gallon sized Ziploc bag.

2. Squeeze out the excess air, seal then label your bag with the ingredients, name of the dish, directions for preparation, and date.

3. Lay flat in your freezer and freeze until you are ready to cook (lasts up to 3 months).

Chicken Santa Fe

Now you can enjoy this delicious chicken dish that is juicy and well seasoned. When ready to cook, simply toss in the pot and top with cheddar cheese when done.

Serves: 3

Time Needed: 10 minutes

Ingredients

- Canned corn (15 oz., whole kernel)
- Chicken breasts (6, halved, deboned and skin removed)
- Canned black beans (15 oz., drained and rinsed)
- Salsa (1 cup, chunky)

Directions

1. Add all your ingredients into a gallon sized Ziploc bag.

2. Squeeze out the excess air, seal then label your bag with the ingredients, name of the dish, directions for preparation, and date.

3. Lay flat in your freezer and freeze until you are ready to cook (lasts up to 3 months).

Jackfruit Stew

This vegetarian stew is rich, and delicious.
Serves: 6

Time: 10 minutes

Ingredients:

- 3lb. jackfruit stew meat, cubed
- 2 garlic cloves, minced
- ½ cup Thai red curry paste
- 2 teaspoons fresh lime juice
- 1/3 cup tomato paste
- 2 cups broccoli florets
- 1 onion, thinly sliced
- 2 garlic cloves, minced
- 2 teaspoons minced ginger
- 1 cup peeled and sliced jicama
- 2 cups shredded carrots

- 2 tablespoons fish sauce
- 14oz. can coconut milk
- 2 tablespoons coconut oil, divided

Directions

1. Add all your ingredients into a gallon sized Ziploc bag.

2. Squeeze out the excess air, seal then label your bag with the ingredients, name of the dish, directions for preparation, and date.

3. Lay flat in your freezer and freeze until you are ready to cook (lasts up to 3 months).

Coconut Chicken Soup

This recipe allows you to achieve the same flavor notes as you would if you were doing everything on the same day.
Serves: 4

Time: 4 hours 20 minutes

Ingredients:

- 0.5lb. roasted chicken carcass
- 14oz. can coconut milk
- 2 tablespoons smooth peanut butter
- ½ purple onion, sliced
- 2 tablespoons fish sauce
- 1 cup sliced shiitake
- 1 lime, juiced
- ¼ red bell pepper, sliced
- 2 tablespoons Thai curry paste
- 2 tablespoon brown sugar

- 1 tablespoon minced ginger
- Salt and pepper, to taste
- 3 cups water

Directions

1. Add all your ingredients into a gallon sized Ziploc bag.

2. Squeeze out the excess air, seal then label your bag with the ingredients, name of the dish, directions for preparation, and date.

3. Lay flat in your freezer and freeze until you are ready to cook (lasts up to 3 months).

Vietnamese Beef Curry Stew

This stew is mouthwatering, and delicious.
Serves: 8

Time: 10 minutes

Ingredients:

- Vegetable oil (2 tbsp.)
- Beef Chuck (750g. trimmed, cubed)
- Onion (1 large)
- Garlic (4 cloves)
- Red Chilies (2)
- Ginger (2 pieces, peeled and grated)
- Curry Powder (2 ½ tbsp.)
- Sugar (2 tsp.)
- Turmeric (2 tsp.)
- Carrots (2, sliced)
- Coconut milk (400 ml)

- Tomatoes (400g, chopped)
- Water (1 cup)
- Fish Sauce (1 tbsp.)

Directions

1. Add all your ingredients into a gallon sized Ziploc bag.

2. Squeeze out the excess air, seal then label your bag with the ingredients, name of the dish, directions for preparation, and date.

3. Lay flat in your freezer and freeze until you are ready to cook (lasts up to 3 months).

Basil Tofu

This dish is fragrant and can be enjoyed on any night of the week.

Serves: 4

Time: 10 minutes

Ingredients:

- 2lb. tofu, extra firm, cubed
- 1 tablespoon fish sauce
- 1 tablespoon lime juice
- 1 red chili pepper, chopped
- 1 teaspoon dried basil
- 2 teaspoons minced garlic
- ½ cup beef broth
- 4oz. baby carrots, peeled
- 5 tablespoons sweet chili sauce

- 4 tablespoons soy sauce
- 1 teaspoon minced ginger

Directions

1. Add all your ingredients into a gallon sized Ziploc bag.

2. Squeeze out the excess air, seal then label your bag with the ingredients, name of the dish, directions for preparation, and date.

3. Lay flat in your freezer and freeze until you are ready to cook (lasts up to 3 months).

Pork Stew

This stew is rich, and delicious.
Serves: 6

Time: 10 minutes

Ingredients:

- 3lb. pork stew meat, cubed
- 2 garlic cloves, minced
- ½ cup Thai red curry paste
- 2 teaspoons fresh lime juice
- 1/3 cup tomato paste
- 2 cups broccoli florets
- 1 onion, thinly sliced
- 2 garlic cloves, minced
- 2 teaspoons minced ginger

- 1 cup peeled and sliced jicama
- 2 cups shredded carrots
- 2 tablespoons fish sauce
- 14oz. can coconut milk
- 2 tablespoons coconut oil, divided

Directions

1. Add all your ingredients into a gallon sized Ziploc bag.

2. Squeeze out the excess air, seal then label your bag with the ingredients, name of the dish, directions for preparation, and date.

3. Lay flat in your freezer and freeze until you are ready to cook (lasts up to 3 months).

Almond Spiced Beef

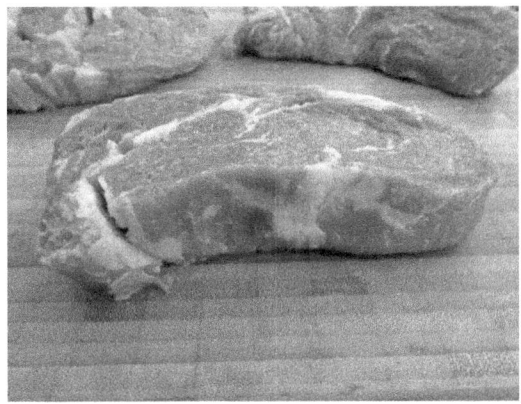

This sweet and salty beef tends to be a hit on any day of the week.

Serves: 6

Time: 10 minutes

Ingredients:

- 2lb. beef, diced
- 2 tablespoons soy sauce
- 5oz. smooth almond butter
- 1 cup beef stock
- 3 tablespoons honey
- 1 tablespoon rice mirin
- 1 tablespoon sesame oil
- 2 tablespoons Thai curry paste

Directions

1. Add all your ingredients into a gallon sized Ziploc bag.

2. Squeeze out the excess air, seal then label your bag with the ingredients, name of the dish, directions for preparation, and date.

3. Lay flat in your freezer and freeze until you are ready to cook (lasts up to 3 months).

Turkey Meatballs

These meatballs remain moist and well-seasoned when cooked.

Serves: 4

Time: 10 minutes

Ingredients:

- 1lb ground turkey
- ½ cup breadcrumbs
- ½ cup beef broth
- 1 ½ cups sweet Thai chili sauce
- 1 egg, beaten
- 2 teaspoons sesame oil
- 2 teaspoons soy sauce
- 3 garlic cloves, minced
- 1 tablespoon sesame seeds

- ½ teaspoon salt

Directions

1. Add your ground turkey, breadcrumbs, egg into a large bowl and stir to combine.
2. Create tablespoon sized balls and place them into a gallon sized Ziploc bag.
3. Add your remaining ingredients to the bag, squeeze out the excess air, seal then label your bag with the ingredients, name of the dish, directions for preparation, and date.
4. Lay flat in your freezer and freeze until you are ready to cook (lasts up to 3 months).

Spicy Chicken Stew

This dish is simple to prepare, and a treat to eat.
Serves: 4

Time: 5 minutes

Ingredients:

- 1lb. boneless chicken thighs
- 1/3 cup soy sauce
- 2 tablespoons minced ginger root
- 2 red bell peppers, sliced
- 3 tablespoons honey
- 6 garlic cloves, minced
- 1/3 cup creamy peanut butter
- 1 teaspoon crushed red pepper flakes

Directions:

1. Add all your ingredients into a gallon sized Ziploc bag.

2. Squeeze out the excess air, seal then label your bag with the ingredients, name of the dish, directions for preparation, and date.

3. Lay flat in your freezer and freeze until you are ready to cook (lasts up to 3 months).

Crockpot Ribs

These ribs are so succulent after its cooked. Best of all, it's simple to cook!

Serves: 6

Time: 10 minutes

Ingredients:

- 3.5lb. pork baby back ribs, cut in half across bones
- 4oz. orange juice concentrate
- 4oz. apple juice concentrate
- 4oz. pineapple juice concentrate
- ¼ cup heavy cream
- ¾ cup soy sauce
- 2 teaspoons palm sugar
- 1 garlic clove, minced
- 4 tablespoons fresh cilantro

Directions

1. Add all your ingredients into a gallon sized Ziploc bag.

2. Squeeze out the excess air, seal then label your bag with the ingredients, name of the dish, directions for preparation, and date.

3. Lay flat in your freezer and freeze until you are ready to cook (lasts up to 3 months).

www.ingramcontent.com/pod-product-compliance
Lightning Source LLC
Chambersburg PA
CBHW071439070526
44578CB00001B/154